HOW CELLS DIVIDE, REPRODUCE, AND SPECIALIZE

ALYSSA SIMON
AND AMY ROMANO

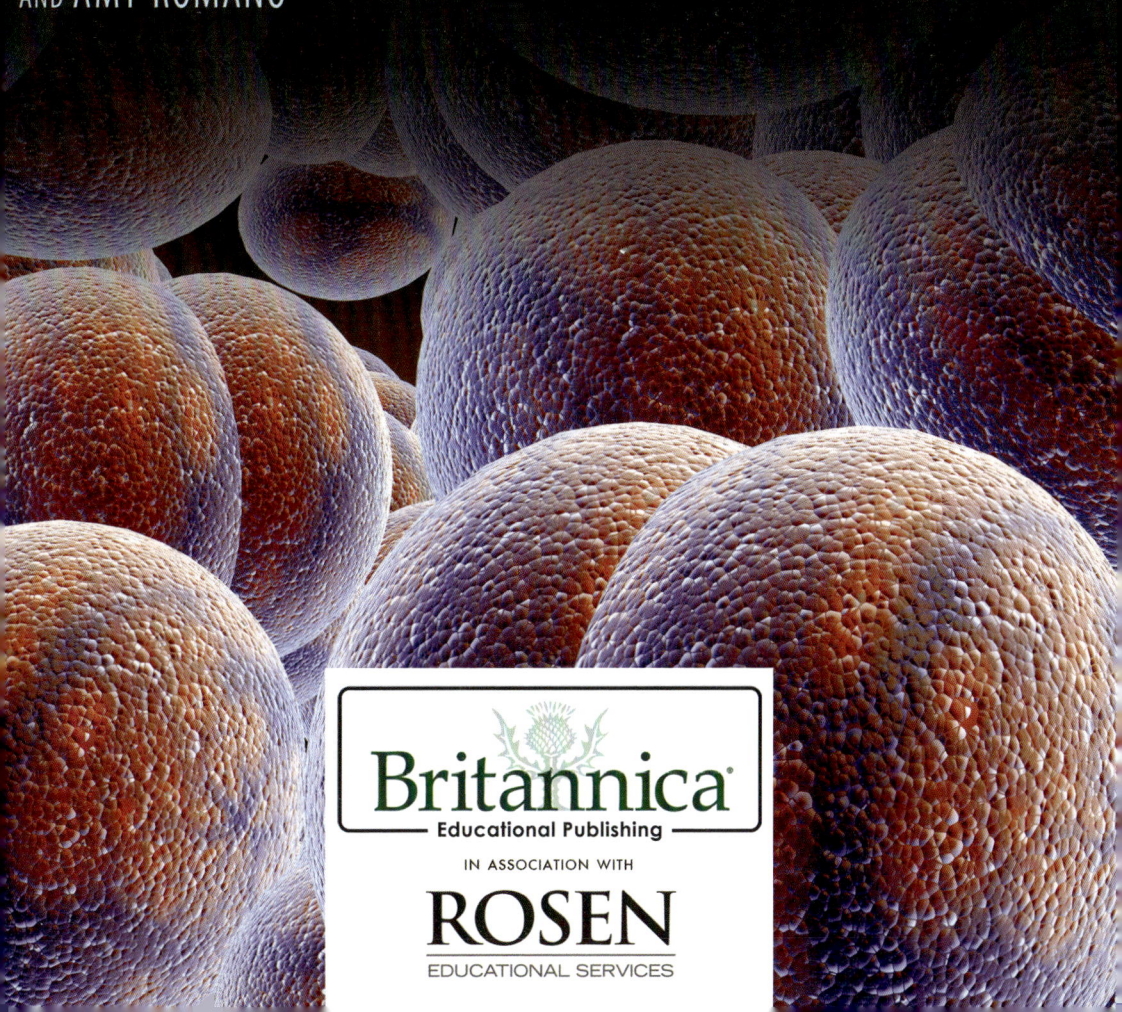

Britannica
Educational Publishing

IN ASSOCIATION WITH

ROSEN
EDUCATIONAL SERVICES

Published in 2015 by Britannica Educational Publishing (a trademark of
Encyclopædia Britannica, Inc.) in association with The Rosen Publishing
Group, Inc.
29 East 21st Street, New York, NY 10010

Distributed exclusively by Rosen Publishing.
To see additional Britannica Educational Publishing titles,
go to rosenpublishing.com.

First Edition

Additional content and editorial input provided by Melissa Petruzzello.

Britannica Educational Publishing
J.E. Luebering: Director, Core Reference Group
Anthony L. Green: Editor, Compton's by Britannica

Rosen Publishing
Hope Lourie Killcoyne: Executive Editor
Tracey Baptiste: Editor
Nelson Sá: Art Director
Michael Moy: Designer
Cindy Reiman: Photography Manager
Karen Huang: Photo Researcher
Introduction and supplementary material by Alyssa Simon

Library of Congress Cataloging-in-Publication Data

Simon, Alyssa, author.
How cells divide, reproduce, and specialize/Alyssa Simon, Amy
Romano.—First edition.
    pages cm.—(The Britannica guide to cell biology)
Includes bibliographical references and index.
ISBN 978-1-62275-802-9 (library bound)
1. Cells—Juvenile literature. 2. Cell physiology—Juvenile literature.
3. Cytology—Juvenile literature. I. Romano, Amy, author. II. Title.
QH582.5.S56 2015
571.6—dc23
                                                                2014020660

Manufactured in the United States of America

Cover: background © Fedorov Oleksiy/shutterstock.com; diagram
silhouetted © iLexx/iStockphoto.com

CONTENTS

INTRODUCTION 4

CHAPTER 1
THE FEATURES OF CELLS. 7

CHAPTER 2
HOW CELLS DIVIDE AND REPRODUCE. 19

CHAPTER 3
SPECIALIZED CELLS 29

CHAPTER 4
ARTIFICIAL SPECIALIZATION 40

GLOSSARY 53

FOR MORE INFORMATION 57

FOR FURTHER READING 60

INDEX. 61

INTRODUCTION

A cell is the smallest unit of living matter that can exist by itself. Known as the "building block of life," every living thing on the planet is made up of at least one cell. Many cells exist as microscopic, unicellular organisms, such as bacteria or yeasts, though other living creatures are composed of multiple cells. An adult human, for example, is made up of about 37.2 trillion individual cells, all of which cooperate in order to carry out vital functions. Despite their small size, cells come in a variety of shapes, ranging from cube-shaped plant cells to disk-shaped red blood cells. Each contains the components that living creatures need to sustain life.

In complex, multicellular organisms, cells combine to form tissues, which in turn make up the organs that compose body systems, such as the respiratory system. In humans, the respiratory system consists of the nasal cavity, throat, voice box, windpipe, bronchi, and lungs, all of which are composed of individual cells. Even the simplest cells are constantly busy performing the processes necessary for life throughout the day. In addition to breathing, cells have a role in digestion of food, reproduction, and growth, among other functions.

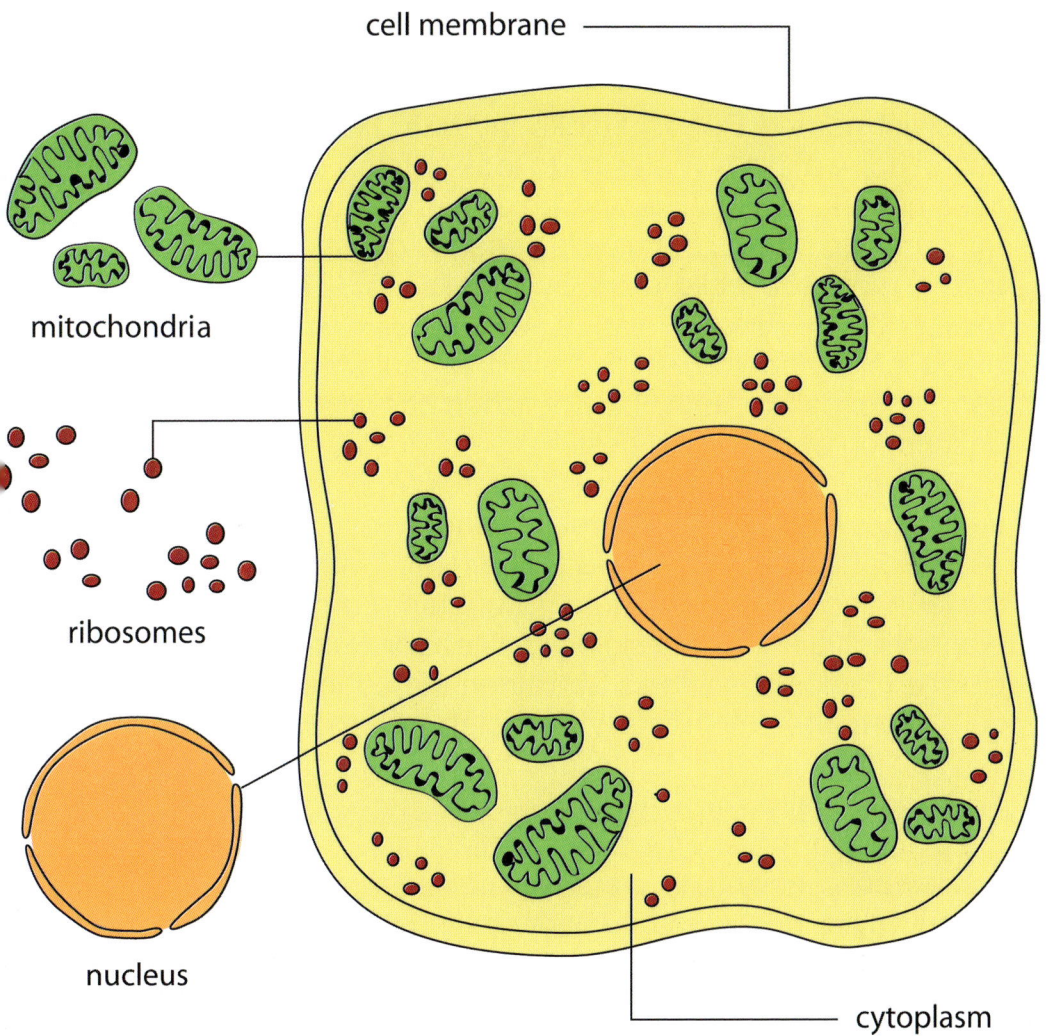

cell membrane

mitochondria

ribosomes

nucleus

cytoplasm

This diagram shows a typical eukaryotic cell. July Store/Shutterstock.com.

The study of cells is a branch of biology called cytology. The scientists who specialize in this field are called
cytologists. Cells were first discovered by an English

physicist named Robert Hooke in 1665. Hooke used a microscope of his own design to look at thinly sliced sections of cork. He saw the tiny, boxlike units that made up the cork and named them cells because of their similarity to the monastic cells used by monks. In 1673, Dutch microscopist Antonie van Leeuwenhoek discovered blood cells and the single-celled organisms, bacteria and protozoa. In 1684, he published the first accurate description of red blood cells.

By the nineteenth century, microscope technology had improved to allow more detailed investigations. In 1831, Scottish botanist Robert Brown discovered the cell nucleus and recognized it as a constant component of plant cells. German physiologist Theodor Schwann and German biologist Mathias Schleiden stated in 1839 that cells were the "elementary particles of organisms" in both plants and animals, an idea now known as cell theory. Additionally, they recognized that some organisms are unicellular while others are multicellular.

However, scientists were still uncertain as to how exactly cells come to be. Early investigators hypothesized that fetal cells develop out of an unformed substance and first develop a nucleus, then the cell body, and finally the cell membrane. It was many years before cytologists understood how cells divide, reproduce, and specialize.

CHAPTER 1

THE FEATURES OF CELLS

Cells come in an astounding variety of shapes and sizes. While most cells are tiny, a few are exceptionally large. A bird's egg, for example, is a single cell yet can be as large as a baseball; some nerve cells can be more than 3 feet (1 meter) long. The variation in cell size and shape is directly related to a cell's function. Skin cells, for example, are flat so that they can pack tightly into layers to protect the body from bacteria, water, and the sun's damaging rays. Muscle cells, on the other hand, are longer and thin and provide movement through patterns of contracting and relaxing. Even single-celled organisms come in a variety of shapes to accommodate their environments.

Eggs, skin, muscle, and nerve cells are all examples of specialized cells. They are each responsible for specific jobs and exist as part of larger organisms. Single-celled organisms, such as amoebas, are self-sufficient and are capable of performing all necessary functions to sustain life on their own. Despite the enormous variety of shapes, sizes, and functions of cells, all cells can be classified into one of two basic groups.

TWO TYPES OF CELLS

All living things can be categorized as being either prokaryotic or eukaryotic. Prokaryotic organisms are unicellular bacteria or archaea and lack a true nucleus and organelles. Instead, their DNA (deoxyribonucleic

Some typical cells

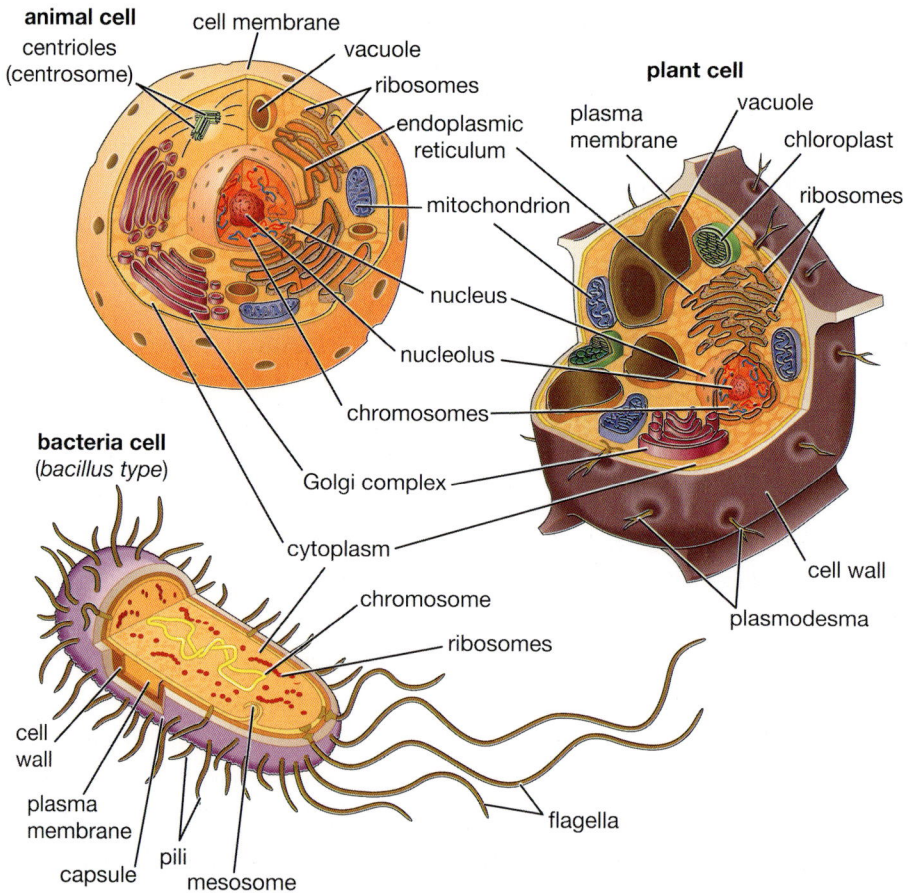

animal cell
centrioles (centrosome)
cell membrane
vacuole
ribosomes
endoplasmic reticulum
mitochondrion
nucleus
nucleolus
chromosomes
Golgi complex
cytoplasm

plant cell
plasma membrane
vacuole
chloroplast
ribosomes
cell wall
plasmodesma

bacteria cell
(*bacillus type*)
chromosome
ribosomes
cell wall
plasma membrane
capsule
pili
mesosome
flagella

© 2012 Encyclopædia Britannica, Inc.

Animal cells and plant cells contain membrane-bound organelles, including a distinct nucleus. In contrast, bacterial cells do not contain organelles. Encyclopædia Britannica, Inc.

acid) floats freely in the cell and many of the cellular tasks are carried out in the membrane that encapsulates the cell. Although they are fairly simple, prokaryotic cells perform extremely complex processes and activities. In fact, prokaryotic cells have a much broader range of biochemical reactions than their relatives, the eukaryotic cells. Eukaryotic cells are generally larger than prokaryotic cells and are more organized and efficient. Eukaryotic cells are found in all multicellular organisms, such as fungi, plants, algae, and animals, and several exist as unicellular organisms, such as paramecia and amoebas. All of the components of eukaryotic cells are housed in a number of interior compartments called organelles. Chief among these is the nucleus, which serves as the cell's control center and contains the chromosomes composed of the cell's double-stranded DNA.

CELL STRUCTURE

Although prokaryotic cells lack the organelles of eukaryotic cells, both cell types feature an outer cell membrane, a jellylike interior known as cytoplasm, DNA, and tiny, bead-like structures called ribosomes.

The cell, or plasma membrane, is a semipermeable wall that allows specific material to leave and enter the cell. Its tiny pores, or openings, permit nutrient and waste molecules to be actively brought into and out of the cell. The cytoplasm is a nutrient-rich fluid that houses the protein-producing ribosomes (and the organelles in eukaryotic cells). DNA is present in all cells and contains the genetically coded instructions for all cell functions, including growth and reproduction.

ORGANELLES

As previously mentioned, eukaryotic organisms conduct their essential functions through the use of organelles in the cytoplasm. The largest organelle is the nucleus, which houses the cell's DNA and thus controls all the

epidermis (skin cells)

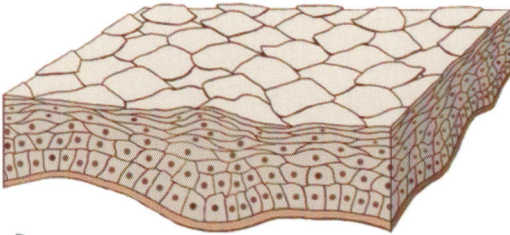

plant cells (root tip)

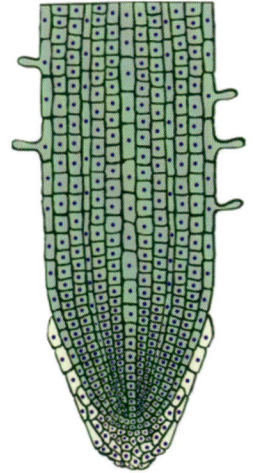

Euglena
(protozoan)

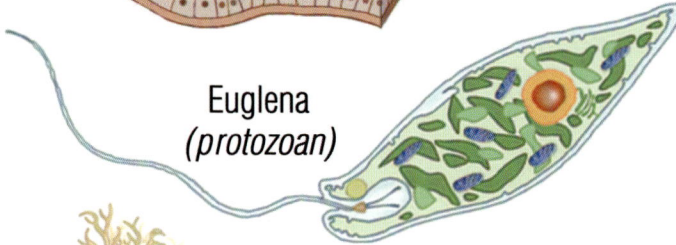

cell body

nerve fiber and cell

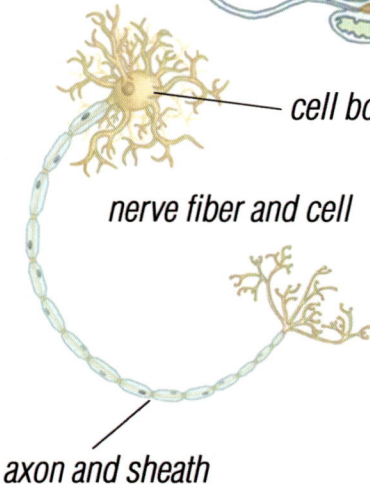

skeletal muscle cells
(muscle fibers)

axon and sheath

These are some examples of eukaryotic cells. Encyclopædia Britannica, Inc.

cell's activities. The nucleus is connected to other organelles through a network of tubes in the cytoplasm. Like the cell itself, the nucleus is surrounded by a porous membrane, part of which is shared by the endoplasmic reticulum.

The endoplasmic reticulum (ER) is a large, membranous organelle, which aids in the synthesis and transport of lipids (fats) and proteins. The rough ER is studded with ribosomes to assist in protein manufacturing. The smooth ER lacks these bumpy ribosomes and is responsible for lipid production. The ER serves somewhat as the cell's circulatory system and keeps proteins and lipids flowing through the cell in an orderly fashion.

Proteins within the cell are largely produced by a number of tiny particles called ribosomes. Ribosomes can be found floating freely in the cytoplasm or embedded in the ER. When a protein needs to be made, messages are sent from the DNA in the cell's nucleus to the ribosomes via a substance known as ribonucleic acid (RNA). RNA is chemically similar to DNA, but only consists of a single strand of sugar instead of two. Two types of RNA, messenger RNA (mRNA) and transfer RNA (tRNA), work together to tell the ribosomes which amino acids need to be combined to form the proteins requested by the nucleus.

Ribosomes also work closely with the Golgi complex, or Golgi apparatus, which stores excess proteins and modifies them as needed. The Golgi complex also packages proteins to be transported wherever they are needed.

Mitochondria are oval-shaped organelles known as the powerhouses of the cell. The mitochondria are where glucose (sugar) and other nutrients are converted into adenosine triphosphate (ATP). The ATP molecule serves as the primary energy source for cellular processes, such as respiration and waste removal.

Chloroplasts are found only in photosynthetic organisms, such as plants and green algae. These organelles serve as the site for photosynthesis and capture the sun's energy to convert water and carbon dioxide into glucose.

Lysosomes and peroxisomes are small organelles that function as the cell's recycling center. They

ENDOSYMBIOTIC THEORY

Mitochondria and chloroplasts are some of the only organelles able to work independently from the cell nucleus. Due to a number of characteristics very similar to the self-sustaining prokaryotes (i.e. no nucleus of its own, similar DNA and ribosomal structure, independent cell division through binary fission, etc.), scientists theorize that mitochondria and chloroplasts may have prokaryotic origins.

The endosymbiosis theory states that millions of years ago, these organelles were free-living prokaryotes. At some point, these prokaryotes were engulfed by other, larger prokaryotes but not digested. Scientists believe this resulted in a symbiotic, or cooperative, relationship.

The cohabitation of these independent cells required that the host cell provide essential nutrients. At the same time, the

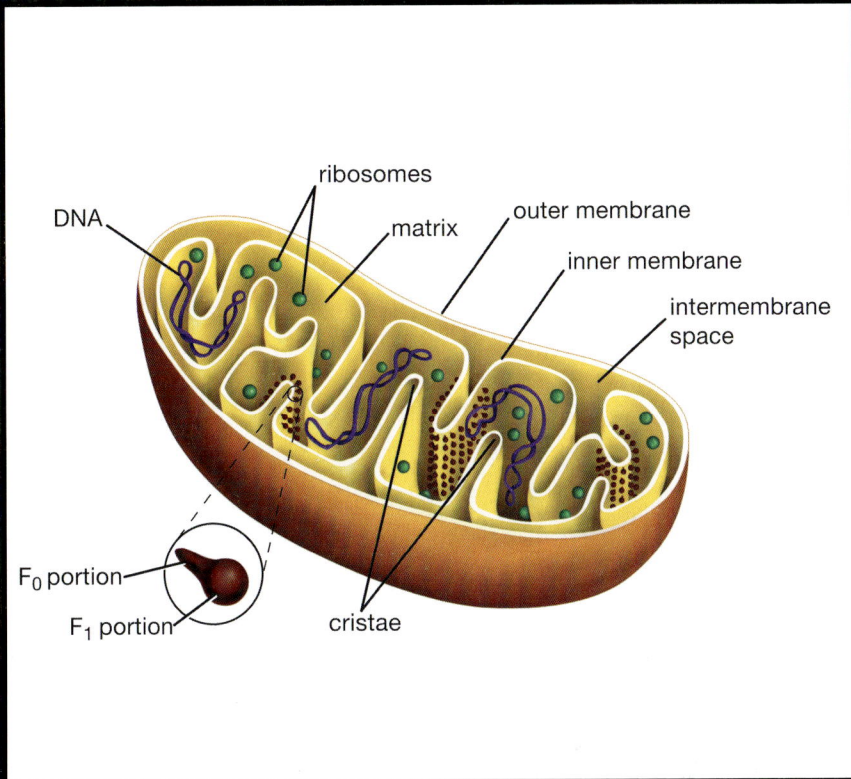

The internal membrane of a mitochondrion is shown here. It is elaborately folded into structures known as cristae. Encyclopaedia Britannica, Inc.

engulfed prokaryotic cell used these nutrients to carry out aerobic respiration or photosynthesis and provide the host cell with an abundant supply of ATP or glucose. Ultimately, it is believed the engulfed cells evolved into what are today known as mitochondria and chloroplasts, which retain the DNA and ribosomal characteristics of their prokaryotic ancestors.

contain enzymes that break down worn-out organelles, unused proteins, lipids, and other molecules the cell recognizes as waste. Centrosomes are organelles that facilitate cell division. They produce microtubules that extend across the cell and help the cell's chromosomes separate during cell division. The centrosome replicates and each moves to opposite ends of the cell before the cell splits.

CELLULAR FOOD AND ENERGY

All cells must obtain or make food to provide the energy necessary for their various processes. Plant and algae cells harness the energy of the sun to make food, while animals and other nonphotosynthetic organisms must obtain their food molecules by consuming plants or other organisms. These food molecules are then broken down into energy to sustain the activities of the cell's organelles and membranes. The cell uses energy to carry out a number of different functions, including recycling molecules, expelling waste, and reproducing. These basic functions enable cells to respond to changes in their environment, adapt accordingly, and continue to live.

PHOTOSYNTHESIS

The process of photosynthesis allows plants and some algae to be self-feeding, or autotrophic. Autotrophs sustain themselves by producing their own food and do not need to eat other organisms. Unlike animal cells, plant and algae cells contain organelles known

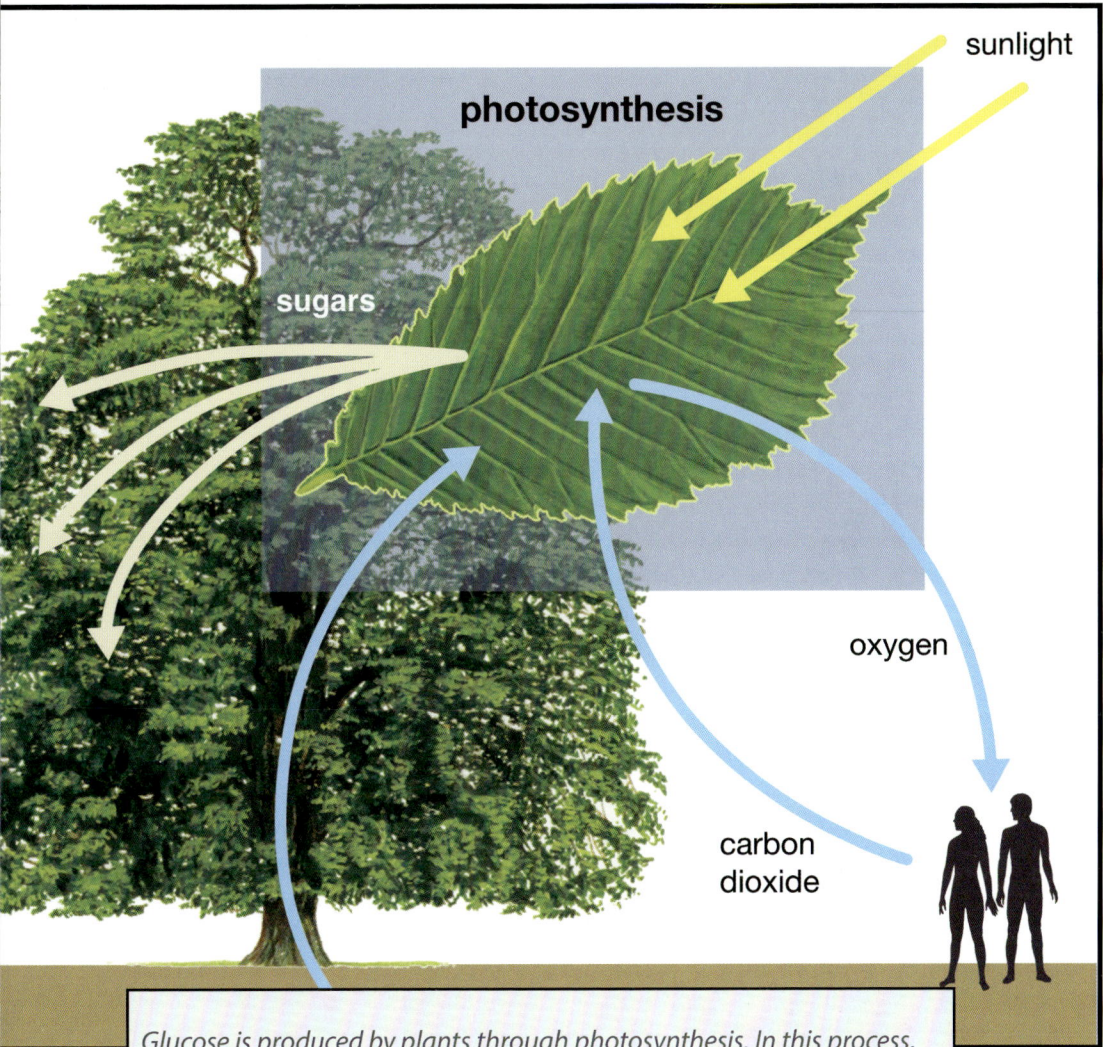

photosynthesis

sunlight

sugars

oxygen

carbon dioxide

Glucose is produced by plants through photosynthesis. In this process, the plant uses light energy from the sun to convert carbon dioxide and water into glucose and oxygen. Encyclopædia Britannica, Inc.

as chloroplasts. These organelles contain a pigment called chlorophyll and serve as the site for photosynthesis. During the process of photosynthesis, the

This emerald green sea slug uses chloroplasts from the algae it eats to make food using the process of photosynthesis. Certain types of bacteria and algae also use photosynthesis. Mary Tyler – Mary Rumpho/University of Maine

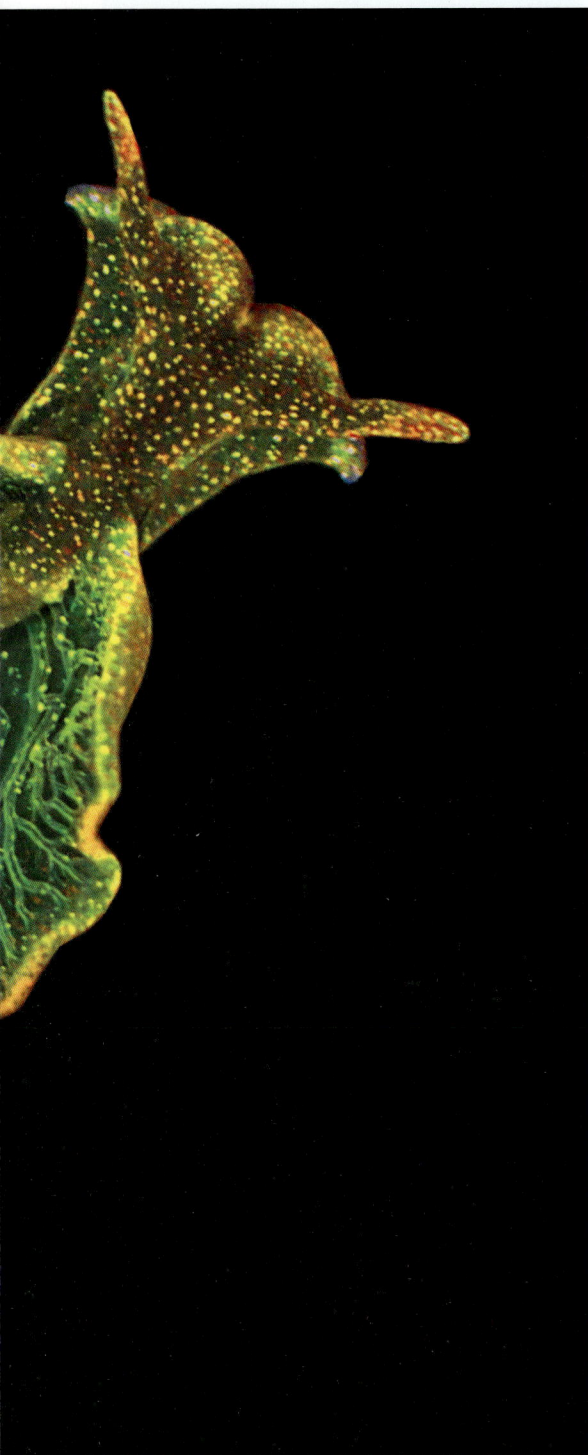

chlorophyll molecules capture energy from the sun and use it to convert water and carbon dioxide into the sugar glucose. Oxygen, which other organisms need to breathe, is released as a by-product of this reaction.

CELLULAR RESPIRATION

While photosynthetic cells can produce their own food, other cells must obtain their foods from outside sources, ranging from simple nutrients dissolved in water and carried into the cell via the plasma membrane to other organisms. Regardless of the source of their food, all cells must convert nutrients into ATP (adenosine triphosphate) in order to use them as energy.

Mitochondria maintain the balance between food and energy. In a typical cell, thousands of ATP molecules are created each second in the mitochondria. Most eukaryotic cells use oxygen to convert glucose (sugar) into ATP through a process known as aerobic (meaning "with oxygen") respiration. Aerobic respiration occurs within a cell constantly. If it ceases, the cell—and ultimately the organism—dies.

ATP molecules can also be created without oxygen through a process called anaerobic (meaning "without oxygen") fermentation. Fermentation is the process by which single-celled eukaryotes such as yeast build ATP.

CHAPTER 2

HOW CELLS DIVIDE AND REPRODUCE

Like all living things, cells have a life cycle that consists of growth, maintenance, and reproduction. The life cycle of most cells consists of two stages. In stage one, the cell grows and performs its vital functions. In stage two, the cell reproduces itself by cell division.

Cell division is different in unicellular and multicellular organisms. In unicellular organisms, cell division is how the organisms reproduce themselves. In multicellular organisms, it is how tissues grow and maintain themselves. While bacteria and archaea usually reproduce themselves through a form of division known as binary fission, most eukaryotic cells divide in a process known as mitosis.

The survival of multicellular eukaryotes depends on how their cells interact. It is essential that a balanced distribution of cells is maintained. Most body tissues grow by increasing their cell number through cell division, though such division more often relates to tissue renewal rather than growth in adult organisms. For example, skin cells are often replaced with new ones after the old, or mature, ones fall off. In other organs, such as the liver, cells divide in order to regenerate following an injury. Some types of cells are prevented from

THE WORK OF DNA

DNA is genetic information found inside every cell. It determines the inherited characteristics of every living thing. It controls how the cell replicates and functions and which traits are inherited from previous generations, such as eye color or blood type.

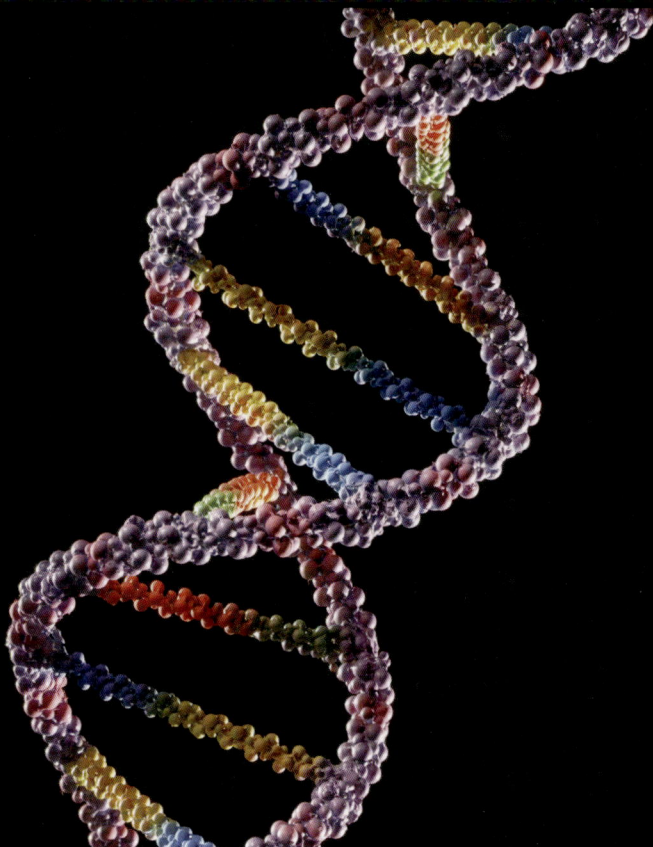

A model of a DNA molecule showing the sugar-phosphate backbone (double helix) and base pairs connecting the two helix spirals.
Comstock/Stockbyte/Thinkstock

The genetic information inside a DNA molecule is organized in sequences called genes. These contain instructions for making proteins, which are needed for growth, repair, and other functions. When cells need to make proteins, instructions sent to its DNA signal an appropriate gene to begin making RNA (ribonucleic acid). The RNA molecule carries the information to a ribosome elsewhere in the cell and serves as a template for the new protein. Errors during this process are a form of genetic mistakes, or mutations.

regenerating and reproducting, including the heart muscle, nerve cells, and lens cells in mammals. The maintenance and repair of these cells is limited to replacing components of the cells themselves, rather than replacing the entire cells.

Whether the purpose is to grow bigger or to repair or replace damaged or dying cells, biologists estimate that approximately 25 million cells in the human body go through some form of cell division every second!

CELL DIVISION: MITOSIS

The simplest method of cell reproduction involves only one parent cell and no specialized parts. In this method, the parent cell divides into two identical pieces, each of which becomes a new cell. This type of reproduction is known as asexual reproduction and usually occurs via a process called mitosis. Nearly all cells in the human body reproduce asexually via mitosis.

Mitosis

Interphase G2

Prophase

Metaphase

Anaphase

Telophase

Cytokinesis

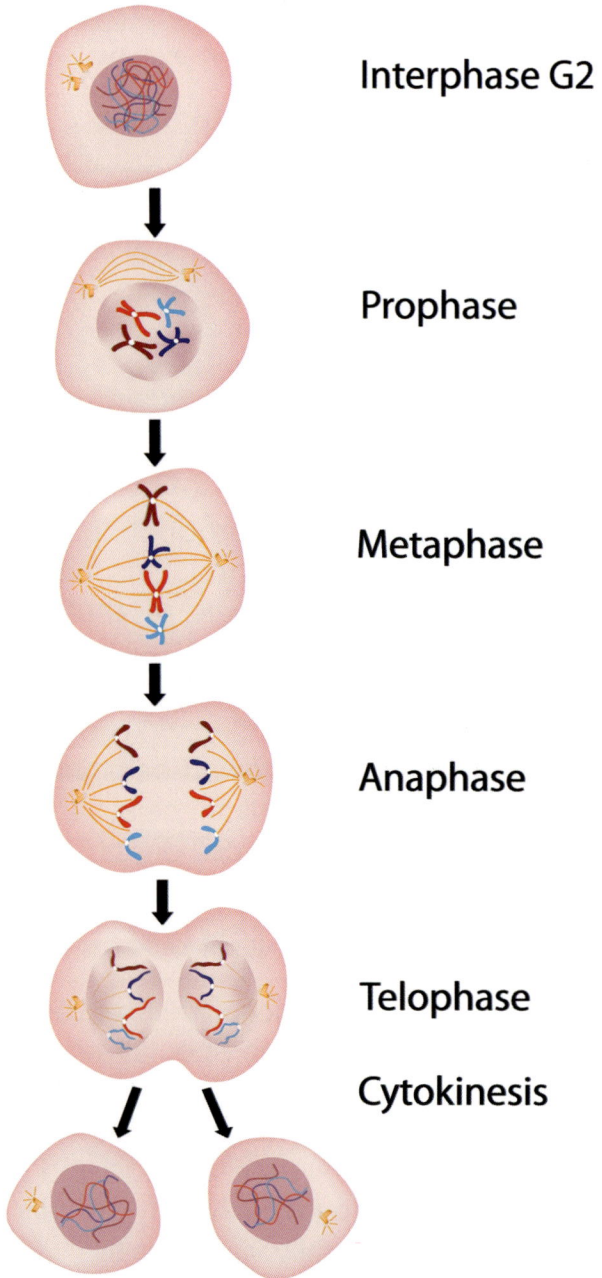

The process of mitosis is continuous, but it can be separated into phases, as shown in this diagram. Alila Medical Media/Shutterstock.com

In mitosis, the nucleus splits in half to form two new "daughter" cells, each with a full set of chromosomes. Mitosis is essential for life to continue and allows multicellular organisms to grow and replace old or damaged cells.

There are five stages of mitosis: prophase, metaphase, anaphase, telophase, and cytokinesis. Interphase is the period between cell divisions, in which cells grow to full size and spend the majority of their lives. The end of interphase consists of the cell making an exact and complete copy of each chromosome (long, threadlike structures composed of DNA and proteins that contain a cell's genetic information) in preparation for mitosis.

PROPHASE

Once the DNA copy is complete, each pair of duplicate chromosomes reorganizes into structures called chromatids. Matching chromatids are joined together at a site known as the centromere. During this stage of mitosis, the nuclear envelope breaks down and the cell forms spindle fibers. The spindle fibers pull the chromatids toward the middle of the cell.

METAPHASE

The still-attached chromatids line up along their centromeres in the middle of the cell.

ANAPHASE

The chromatid pairs split apart at the centromere to form two identical chromosomes. Each half of the pair moves along the spindle fibers to opposite sides (poles) of the cells.

TELOPHASE

The chromosomes have reached the opposite poles of the cell, the spindle disappears, the nuclear membrane forms again, and the chromosomes expand into thin strands of chromatin (a complex of DNA and various proteins).

CYTOKINESIS

Once the division of the nucleus is complete, the cytoplasm divides. The cell membrane contracts and pinches the cell between the two nuclei until the cytoplasm separates into two new daughter cells. Mitosis ends with the formation of two new cells, each with a matching and complete set of chromosomes, as well as an identical composition of cellular structures.

Although it is a simple, reliable way of dividing and multiplying, mitosis has one very important disadvantage: the lack of genetic variability. The daughter cells never obtain any new characteristics and may require a longer period to adapt to environmental changes or to fight disease. This inability to adapt is the reason most animals, including humans, reproduce sexually, not asexually.

SEXUAL REPRODUCTION

Sexual reproduction has the advantage of combining genetic information so that the next generation can have more variation. Organisms are more likely to survive if they have the ability to adapt to changing environments. Gametes, or sex cells, are created for sexual reproduction through the process of meiosis. In humans and many other animals, female eggs are produced in the ovaries and male sperm are produced in the testes. These gametes have half of the chromosomes of the other cells in the body. When sexual reproduction occurs, a gamete joins with another gamete to produce a new cell with a full and unique set of chromosomes. The resulting zygote is a new cell with the potential to transform itself into a highly complex organism and may specialize into billions of different cells.

During meiosis, a special parent cell, known as a germ cell, undergoes two sets of divisions. The result is four new daughter cells, called haploid cells, each with half the total number of chromosomes of the parent cell. These two divisions are known as meiosis I and meiosis II.

MEIOSIS I

Meiosis I is very similar to mitosis and consists of the stages prophase I, metaphase I, anaphase I, and telophase I. The chromosomes of a diploid cell (a cell with a full set of chromosomes) duplicate and join in pairs. The paired chromosomes (each called a tetrad) align at the center of the cell and exchange genetic material in a process known as recombination, or crossing over. The pairs then separate and move to opposite poles in the cell. The cell then splits to form two daughter cells, each of which contains a haploid (half) set of chromosomes that consist of duplicate chromatids.

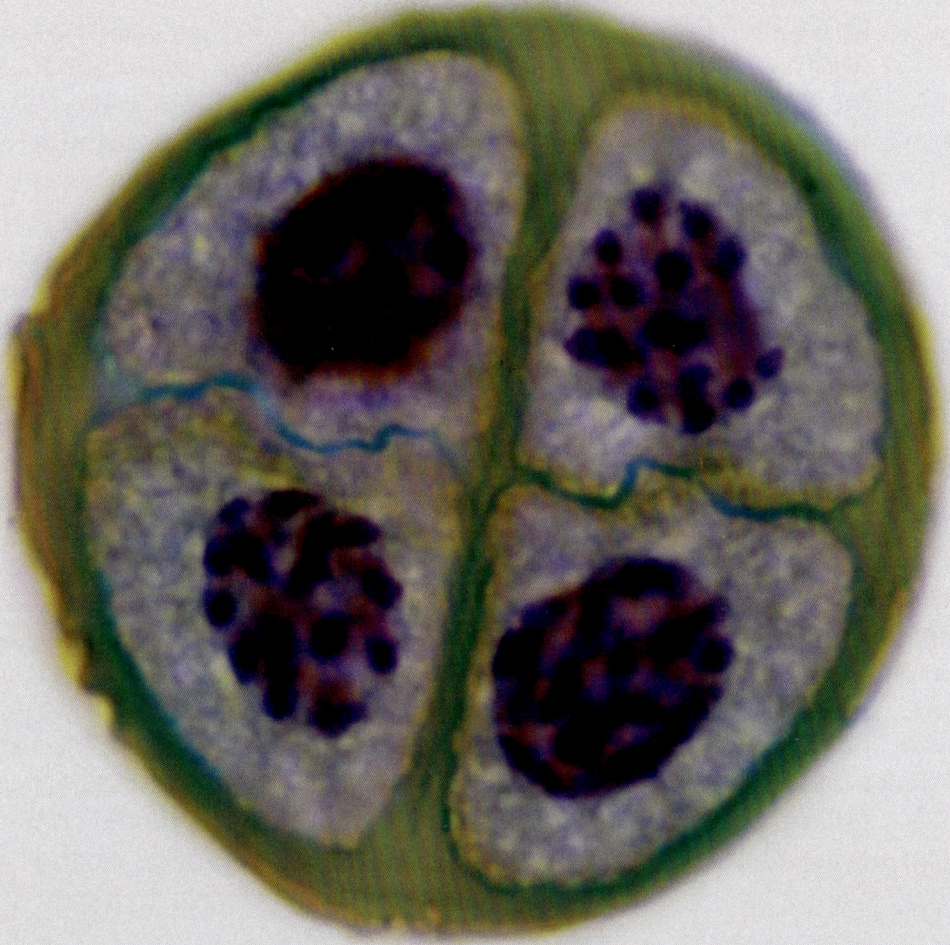

During meiosis II, the four daughter haploid cells contain half the chromosomes of the mother cell. Ed Reschke/Photolibrary/ Getty Images

MEIOSIS II

As meiosis proceeds, the two daughter cells undergo another cell division to form a total of four haploid cells. Meiosis II consists of prophase II, metaphase II, anaphase II, and telophase II. There is no interphase in meiosis II because the chromosomes of the daughter cells are not copied again. Unlike meiosis I, there is no reduction in chromosome number during this division.

Meiosis Overview

homologous pair of chromosomes

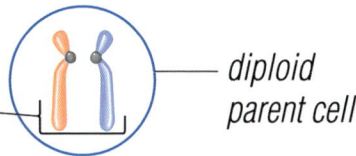

diploid parent cell

chromosomes replicate

homologous pair of replicated chromosomes

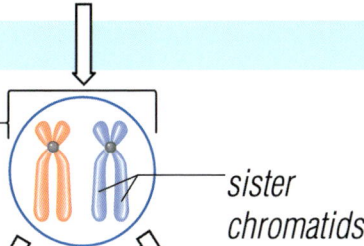

sister chromatids

first cell division

homologous pair of replicated chromosomes separate

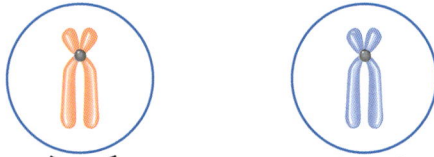

second cell division

sister chromatids separate

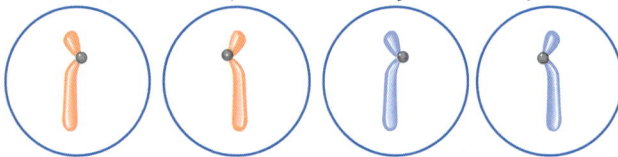

four haploid daughter cells

Meiosis begins with a diploid germ cell that undergoes two sets of divisions to produce four, haploid daughter cells, known as gametes.
Encyclopædia Britannica, Inc.

Meiosis II involves only the separation of each chromatid pair into chromosomes, which are then pulled to the opposite ends of the daughter cells.

In the case of male animals, the four haploid cells differentiate into sperm, most of which are equipped with a whiplike flagellum "tail" to enable movement. In female animals, one of the four haploid cells results in a large egg called an ovum and the remaining three form smaller "polar bodies" that usually die off. This unequal division occurs so that the egg receives the majority of the cytoplasm of the original germ cell in order to support its growth if it is fertilized.

CHAPTER 3

SPECIALIZED CELLS

All multicellular organisms begin life as a single fertilized egg cell, known as a zygote. This cell multiplies using the process of mitosis and develops into a complex organism, potentially composed of billions of cells. The embryonic cells of a developing organism specialize to form its various tissues and organs. The key to such specialization is in the genes, which produce special proteins to regulate the expression of the genetic blueprint.

The human body consists of more than 200 different types of cells, many of which are modified to carry out a particular function. These cells are called specialized cells and have structural adaptations that help them do their respective jobs. For example, red blood cells transport oxygen from the lungs to all of the body's tissues, while nerve cells transmit signals to and from the brain.

All cells in a multicellular organism have the same set of chromosomes that contains the instructions for the entire organism. However, as embryonic cells divide, certain genes within the cells' DNA are activated and others remain dormant. Genes control the production of protein, and different proteins result in different cellular characteristics. This process of specialization is referred to as differentiation. Undifferentiated cells are known as stem cells and have the potential to specialize into any of the body's various cells.

Differentiation in eukaryotic cells often depends on the presence or absence of molecules called transcription factors. These factors influence the fundamental level of gene control. They may function as activators or enhancers, in effect, turning certain genes on or off.

HOW CELLS MULTIPLY AND SPECIALIZE

The zygote is the union of the egg and sperm, which have fused together to form the nucleus of the zygote. As the zygote develops, its cells specialize into tissues and organs based on the instructions of their activated genes. Each gene produces special proteins to regulate the expression of the genetic blueprint.

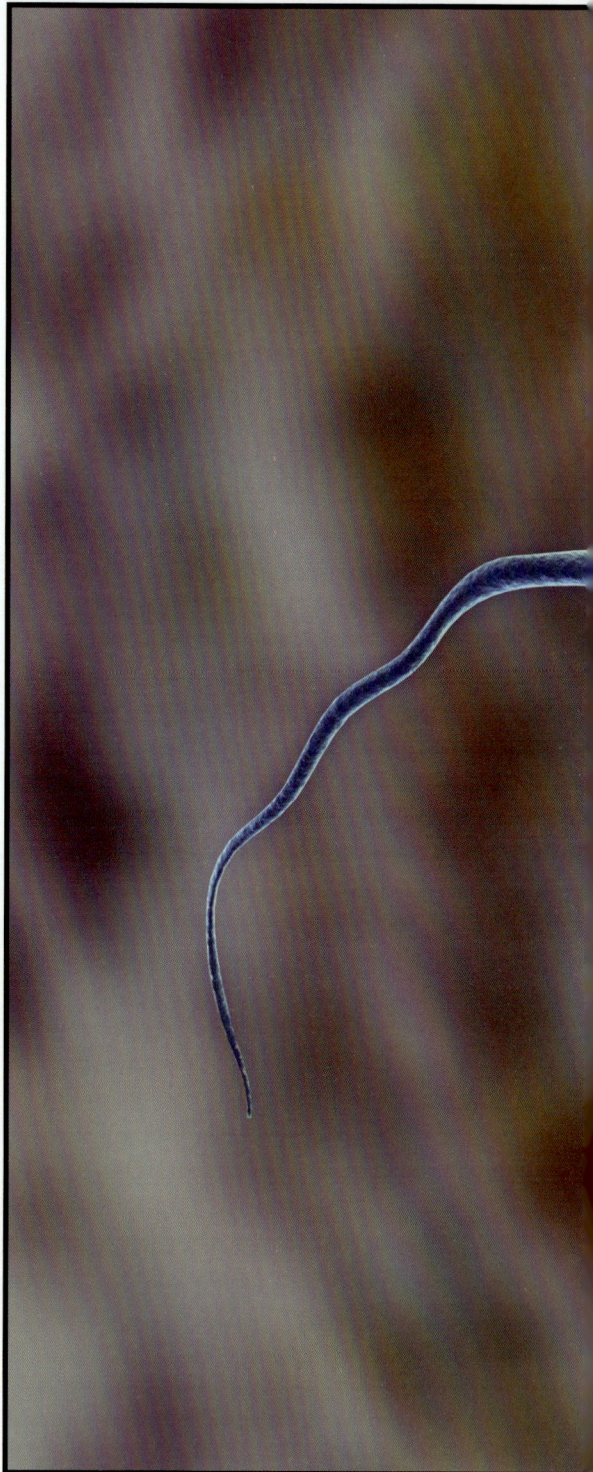

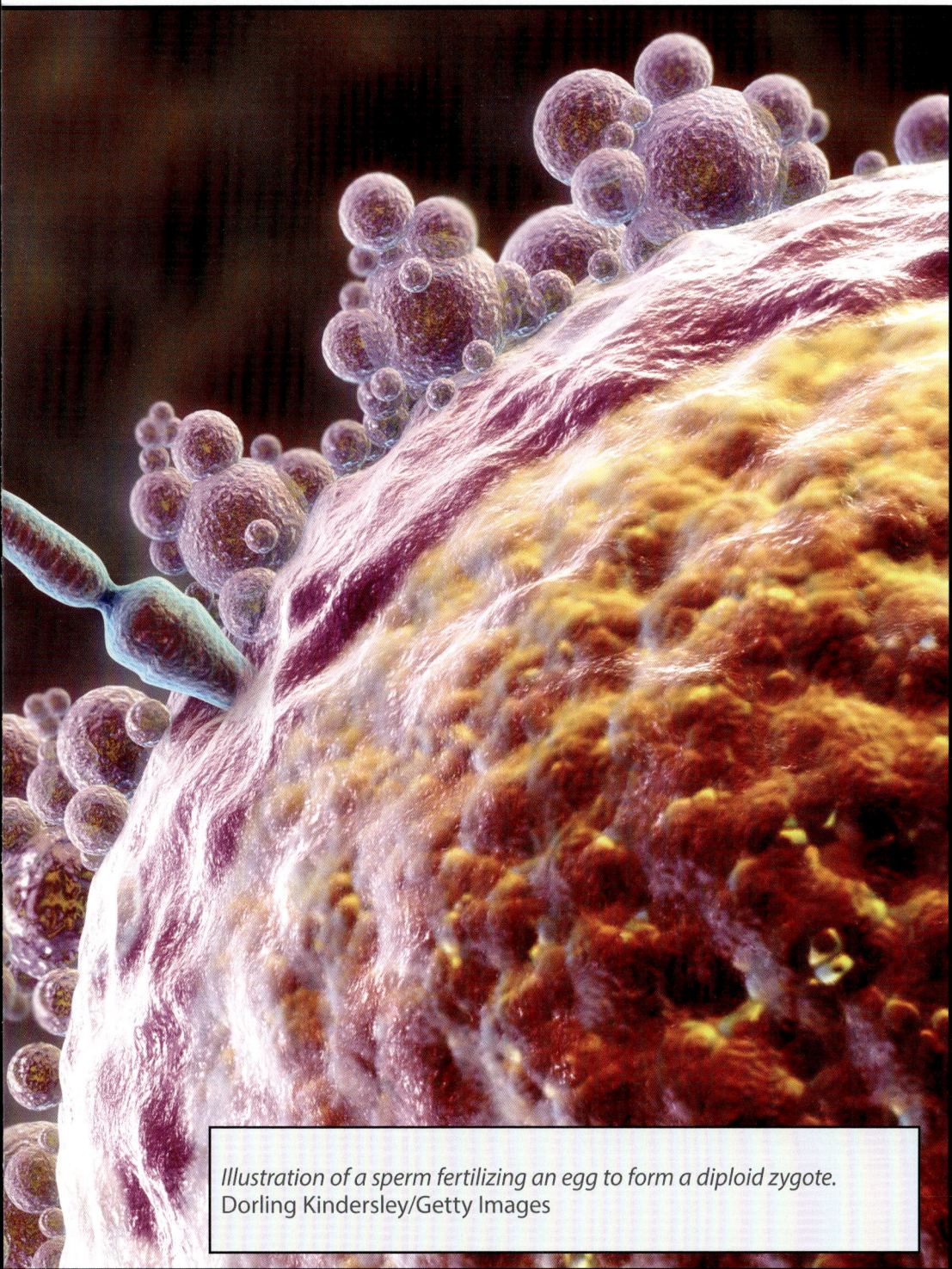

Illustration of a sperm fertilizing an egg to form a diploid zygote.
Dorling Kindersley/Getty Images

DIFFERENTIATED CELLS

Cell differentiation and regulation occur as soon as the single-celled zygote divides for the first time. As stated previously, it is believed that all of an organism's genes are present in each cell nucleus, no matter what the cell type. The differences between tissues are thus not due to the presence or absence of certain genes but are due to the expression of some and the repression of others. Genes that are expressed trigger the production of

Specialized cells in higher plants

leaf cells

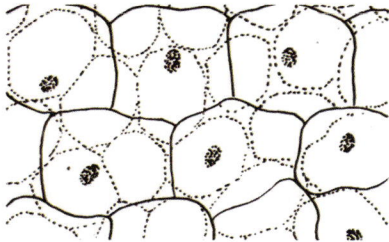

stem cells

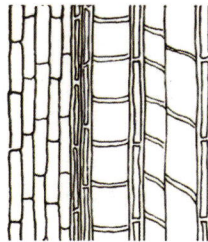

root cells

Specialized cells in higher animals

muscle cells

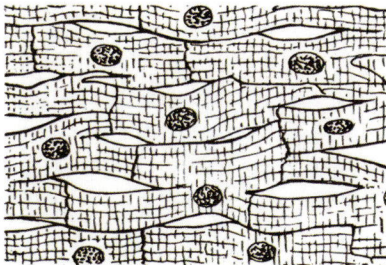

nerve cells

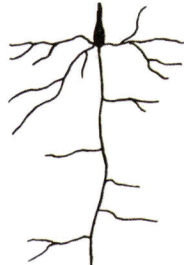

intestine cells

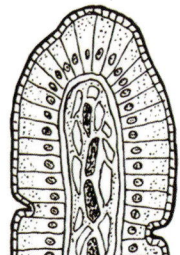

© 2011 Encyclopædia Britannica, Inc.

Higher plants have specialized kinds of cells. Some leaf cells have chlorophyll for making food. Stem cells stiffen the plant. Root cells take in water and minerals. Higher animals also have specialized cells. However, they cannot make food from lifeless materials as plants do. Encyclopædia Britannica, Inc.

specific proteins known as enzymes. These enzymes, in turn, control the cell's synthesis of a particular set of proteins, carbohydrates, and lipids, which ultimately dictate how the cell will differentiate and specialize. Different genes are expressed at different stages of an embryo's development to control its growth and organization. If genes are improperly expressed or remain inactivated when they should be active, mutations can occur.

Within the embryo, the cells do not exist independently of each other. Whether a gene is active or not is sometimes the result of an interaction between cells. Cells often develop differently in different locations of the embryo, most likely because of cell-to-cell communication. The messages they send have the power to transform both the appearance and roles of other cells. One cell, for example, might tell its neighbor to focus on making a particular type of protein. When that cell divides, the daughter cells also make that protein and then signal their neighbors to make more of it. This process is called induction, and it plays a very important role in the early stages of embryonic development.

One example of induction can be observed early on in human embryo development. On the sixth day after fertilization, the embryo is made up of about 120 cells. Through the process of induction, groups of cells join together to make enzymes to help implant the embryo in the mother's uterine wall.

DEVELOPMENT OF ANIMAL EMBRYOS

Scientists divide the development of animal embryos into three different stages: called cleavage, gastrulation, and organogenesis.

CLEAVAGE

Cleavage officially begins when the zygote starts to divide. Although there are a number of divisions during this phase, the embryo doesn't increase in size. This is because the cells skip over the normal growth phase between divisions. Each time there is a division, the daughter cells decrease in size.

As this point, the cluster of cells is still the same size as the original zygote and looks somewhat like two balls of cells. The place where those two balls are pressed up against each other is where the embryo will form. One ball is the yolk sac (loaded with fat and protein that provides nutrition to organisms that grow in eggs or seeds). The other ball will eventually become the amniotic sac, a fluid-filled "bag," which protects the growing organism from bumps and jolts throughout its development.

GASTRULATION

During gastrulation, the ball of cells is transformed into a multilayered organism with recognizable cell differentiation. In humans, this occurs about two weeks after fertilization. While this phase may occur at different times in different organisms, the movement and organization of cells is remarkably similar among organisms ranging from flies to fish to humans.

The most important activity is the transformation of cells into the beginnings of the embryo. The embryo will have three distinct layers: the external ectoderm, the internal endoderm, and the intermediate mesoderm.

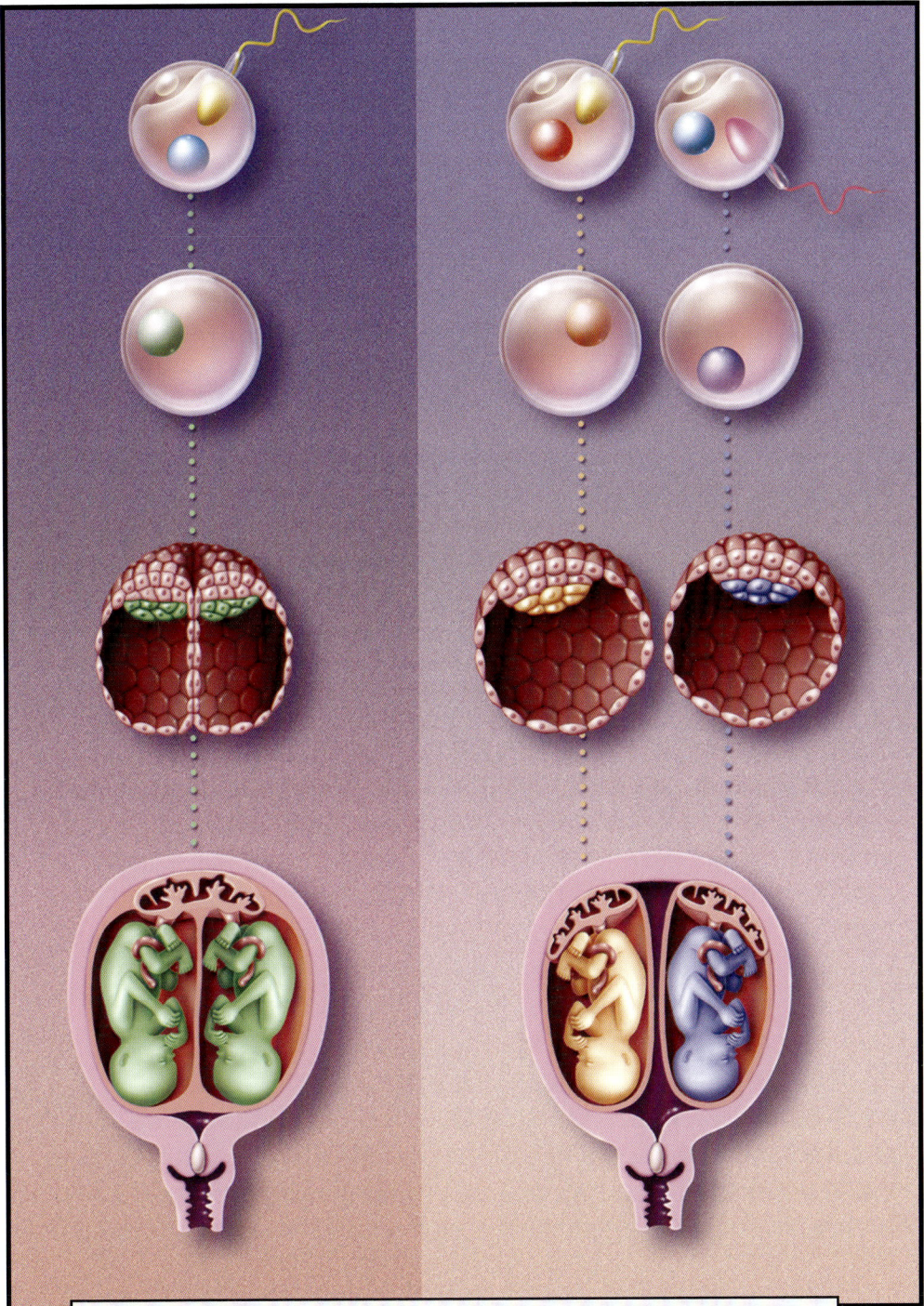

This diagram illustrates the difference between the development of embryos that will become identical twins (left) and fraternal twins (right). BSIP/Science Source

The cells that line the inside of the embryo are called the endoderm. Those cells will eventually become the animal's digestive tract, as well as other internal organs. The cells layered on the outside of the embryo will become the organism's ectoderm, including the skin, nervous system, and parts of the eye and inner ear. The third layer, located between the endoderm and ectoderm, is the mesoderm. "Meso" in mesoderm is defined as "middle" and it is in this layer that the heart, muscles, bones, blood, and sex organs will develop.

ORGAN FORMATION

With the three layers in place as a foundation, the embryo can begin building actual organs. This process is called organogenesis. As the embryonic cells divide, the daughter cells assume forms and functions different from the mother cell. In some cases, the two daughter cells will form altogether different tissues or organs.

Some cells are programmed to function for a short period, then self-destruct. This process is called programmed cell death, or apoptosis. Human embryos—like all embryos with a backbone or vertebrae, start out with tails and webbed hands and feet. Six weeks into development, those cells are sent "death signals," which cause the cells to die. This leaves the embryo without a tail and with recognizable and distinct fingers and toes.

The yolk of the fertilized egg fuels this process for most animals. Mammal growth is more complex and requires more energy than the yolk can provide. Early in its development, the embryo plants itself in the mother's uterine wall. There, the embryo forms a direct connection

EVOLUTIONARY LINKS

Early development of embryos reveals a fascinating fact. About four weeks after fertilization, vertebrate animal embryos possess a clearly defined head and the beginnings of arm and leg "buds." These projections will later develop into limbs. What's amazing is that at this stage it is almost impossible to tell the difference between various animal embryos.

A four-week-old human embryo looks very much like a cat or pig or chicken embryo. All of them have not only tails, but gill pouches, which will develop into gills in fish. In humans, the tail will shrink and those gills will develop into parts of the human face.

This similarity hints at the evolutionary links between all life-forms. It also points out that while genetic information might not be finally expressed, it's still there lurking in the background. In a fish embryo, the genes that control gill development can still be triggered. Scientists think that in humans, those genes are either absent, inactive, or have evolved into something else.

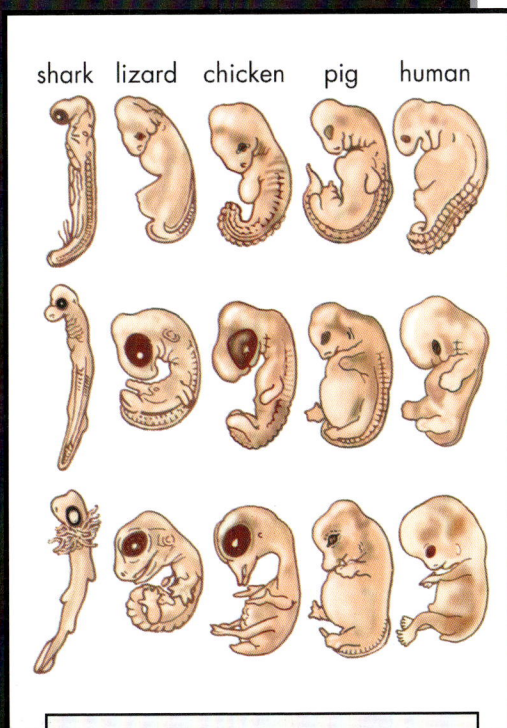

shark lizard chicken pig human

The embryos of many animals appear similar to one another in the earliest stages of development and progress into their specialized forms in later stages. Encyclopædia Britannica, Inc.

with the mother's blood supply, where it can receive essential nutrients.

DEVELOPMENT OF PLANT EMBRYOS

Like animals, many plants reproduce by the coming together of an egg and a sperm. When the plant zygote forms, it triggers cell division and development of

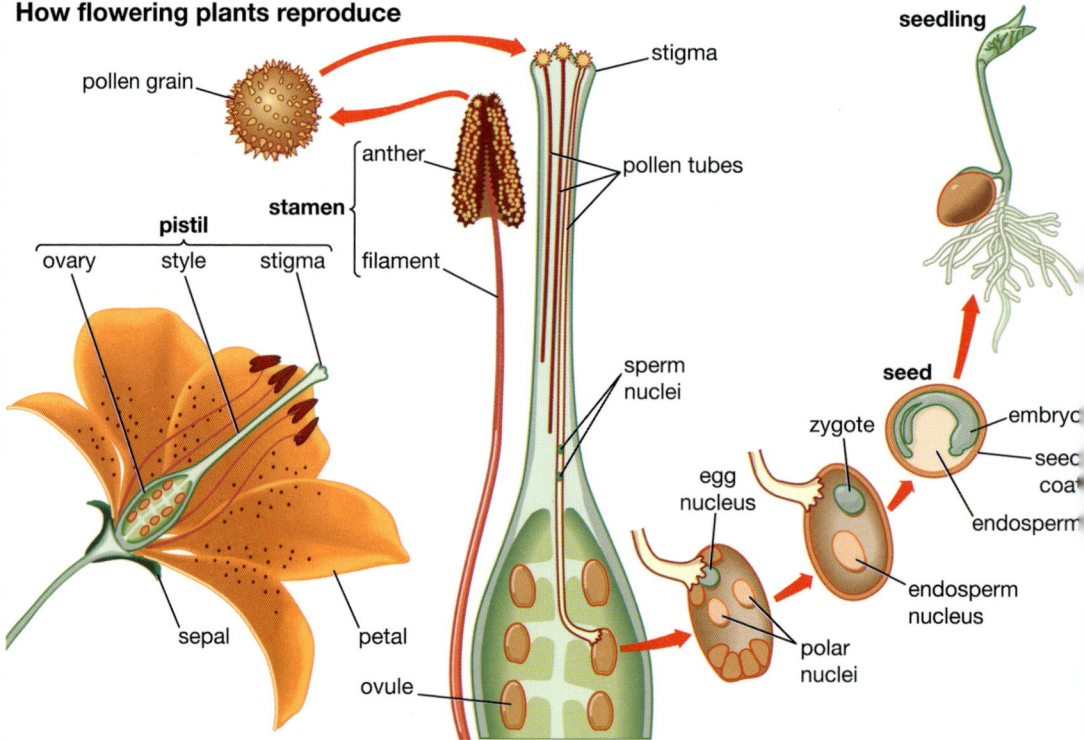

How flowering plants reproduce

pollen grain

stigma

anther

pollen tubes

stamen

pistil

ovary   style   stigma   filament

sperm nuclei

egg nucleus

zygote

seed

embryo

seed coat

endosperm

endosperm nucleus

polar nuclei

sepal   petal

ovule

seedling

Reproduction in flowering plants begins with pollination, the transfer of pollen to a flower's stigma. Encyclopædia Britannica, Inc.

the embryo. A seed is very much like an egg. Inside it is an embryo, which has the potential to grow into a plant.

Plant embryology is similar to animal embryology, but there are distinct differences. Plants have different systems, and scientists use different terminology to explain their reproductive process. For example, plant embryos are not born, they "germinate" from a seed.

Growth is another big difference between plants and animals. At some point animals mature and stop growing. Certain parts of plants, however, remain in the embryonic phase. For example, a plant's roots and shoots continue to grow throughout its life.

CHAPTER 4

ARTIFICIAL SPECIALIZATION

In 1995, the Nobel Prize in Medicine was awarded to three biologists for their discovery of individual genes that control the position of different body parts. It was their hope that by isolating and studying these genes, they could someday help children born with limb deformities or victims of amputation by using living limbs instead of prosthetics.

As research continued, scientists developed a better understanding of how cells work. In 2014, the E. B. Wilson Medal, the highest scientific honor of the American Society of Cell Biology, went to three scientists whose work on the cytoskeleton, the cell's framework, identified how cells can influence life and disease. They found that a certain form of kidney disease was caused by dysfunctional, nonmoving cells, which led to discoveries of other diseases due to this cell defect.

Although cell research has brought fascinating developments, there is plenty of controversy surrounding cell manipulation, especially with regard to human beings. At the center of the controversy is the process of cloning (the artificial production of an organism genetically identical to its parent) and stem cell research (the study and manipulation of undifferentiated cells).

STEM CELLS

Most of the cells in multicellular organisms begin as stem cells. Stem cells contain the instructions needed to make the cell differentiate. Scientists are working to instruct stem cells to grow in particular ways. If successful, this research could lead to treatments for many conditions and diseases.

The most useful types of stem cells come from embryos (organisms that are still at a very early stage of development). Human embryos are sometimes created in a laboratory as part of a process to help infertile people have children. Some of these unused embryos are donated for use in research. Scientists can also get stem cells by cloning, or copying, cells as well as from umbilical cords and from certain tissues in adults.

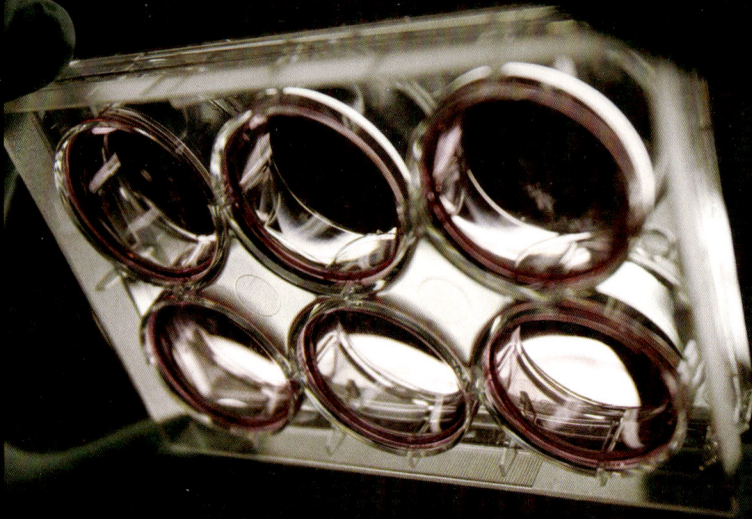

Although cloning occurs naturally, as in the development of twins, artificial cloning has caused controversy. Sandy Huffaker/Getty Images

CELL MEMORY

Scientists have discovered that cells are packed full of genetic memories. In one experiment, researchers transplanted some pancreas cells into the brain. After the transplant, the cells "remembered" that they were pancreatic cells. They continued to make pancreatic hormones.

However, the experiment also showed that cells can be influenced by their environment. When those same pancreatic cells were placed in a test tube outside of the body, they behaved differently. Away from the organism, they forget their specialty. Many of them reverted to the blob shape and behavior of single-celled amoebas. When the specialized cell was placed back in its proper environment, its memory kicked in and it resumed its old functions.

This plasticity of behavior led to further tests by scientists, who discovered that stem cells contain instructions to make the cell grow into a specialized type, such as a muscle, nerve, or blood cell. Once believed to be available only in embryos, scientists have recently discovered that adults have stem cells that can specialize the same way that the cells of embryos can.

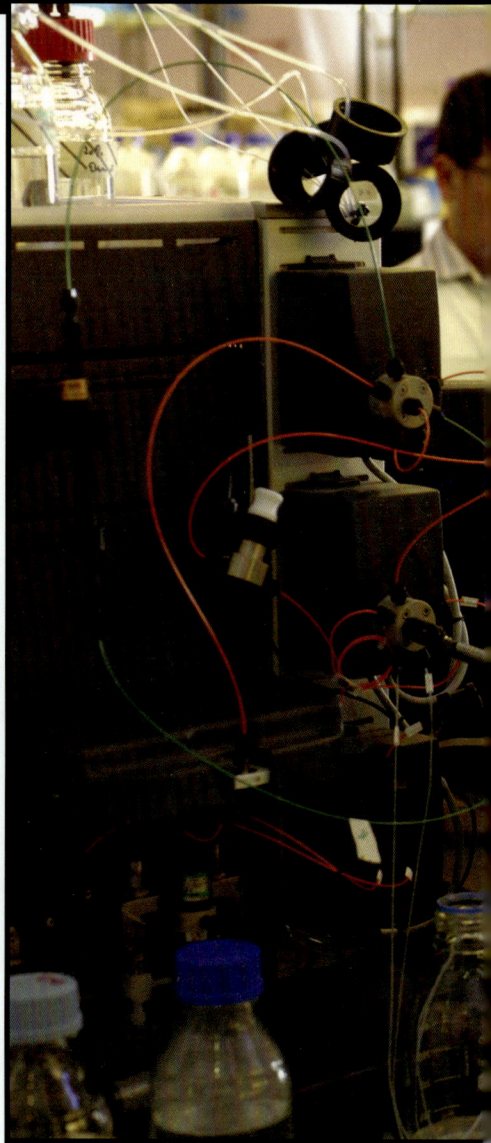

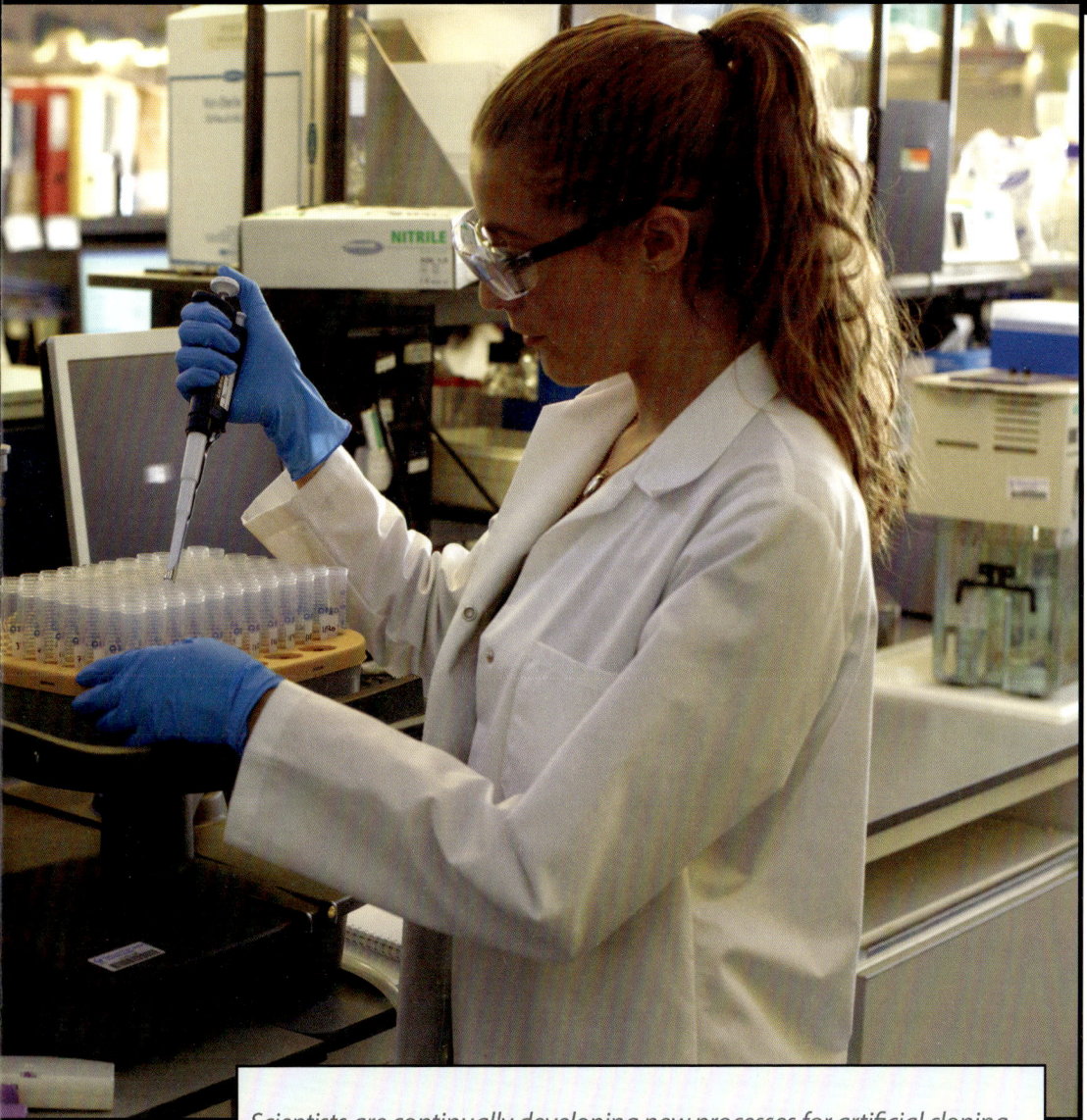

Scientists are continually developing new processes for artificial cloning.
Jonathan Bird/Photolibrary/Getty Images

Scientists are now working on the idea that a stem cell can be instructed to grow into specific types of cells, which could be used to replace damaged tissue in a patient. The results could potentially mean new treatments for diseases such as Alzheimer's disease, Parkinson's disease, and heart disease, and could even repair damaged spinal cords. Although scientists have a long way to go before they have a complete understanding of how cells are reproduced and regulated, we are well on our way to comprehending these impressive and complex biological processes and harnessing the information in them for use in the treatment of disease.

ARTIFICIAL CLONING

Although cloning occurs naturally in both plants and animals during mitosis or the development of multiples such as identical twins, the controlled or guided process of cloning is still being developed by scientists. This artificial cloning has been met with some ethical challenges. Questions about the

This starfish is regenerating its arms. This is an example of naturally occuring cloning. Peter Dazeley/Iconica/Getty Images

morality and societal implications of human cloning have spurred fiery debates in a number of political, religious, and medical forums. Advocates argue that cloning may be key in the treatment of a number of diseases, as cloned human cells could be used in regenerative medicine and provide tissues and organs for transplantation without the need for immunosuppressing drugs. Additionally, cloning may provide a way for defective genes to be replaced, thus reducing or eliminating many genetic diseases and mutations.

Artificial cloning began when scientists began controlling the process of mitosis. Later, they used animal embryos in their experiments and were able to control the cellular development of an organism from a fertilized egg to create an exact, full-grown copy.

Then, in the 1950s, scientists experimented with undifferentiated embryonic cells from animals. These undifferentiated cells are derived from an embryo at a very early stage of development and are totipotent (able to give rise to a complete organism). To exploit this cellular flexibility, scientists developed three techniques to clone embryonic cells: blastomere separation, blastocyst division, and somatic cell nuclear transfer.

BLASTOMERE SEPARATION

In blastomere separation, an egg cell is fertilized with a sperm cell in a laboratory dish. The embryo is allowed to divide until it forms a mass of about four cells. Scientists then remove the outer coating of the embryo and place it in a special solution. This solution encourages the individual cells of the embryo, known as blastomeres, to separate. Each blastomere is then put in a culture where it forms another embryo containing the same genetic makeup as the original. Each new embryo can then be implanted into the uterus of a surrogate mother and is able to develop as any other embryo would.

BLASTOCYST DIVISION

Blastocyst division differs slightly from blastomere separation in that scientists allow a fertilized egg to divide until it forms a mass of about 32 to 150 cells, known as a blastocyst. The researchers then split the blastocyst in two parts and implant both halves into the uterus of a surrogate mother. The two halves develop as identical

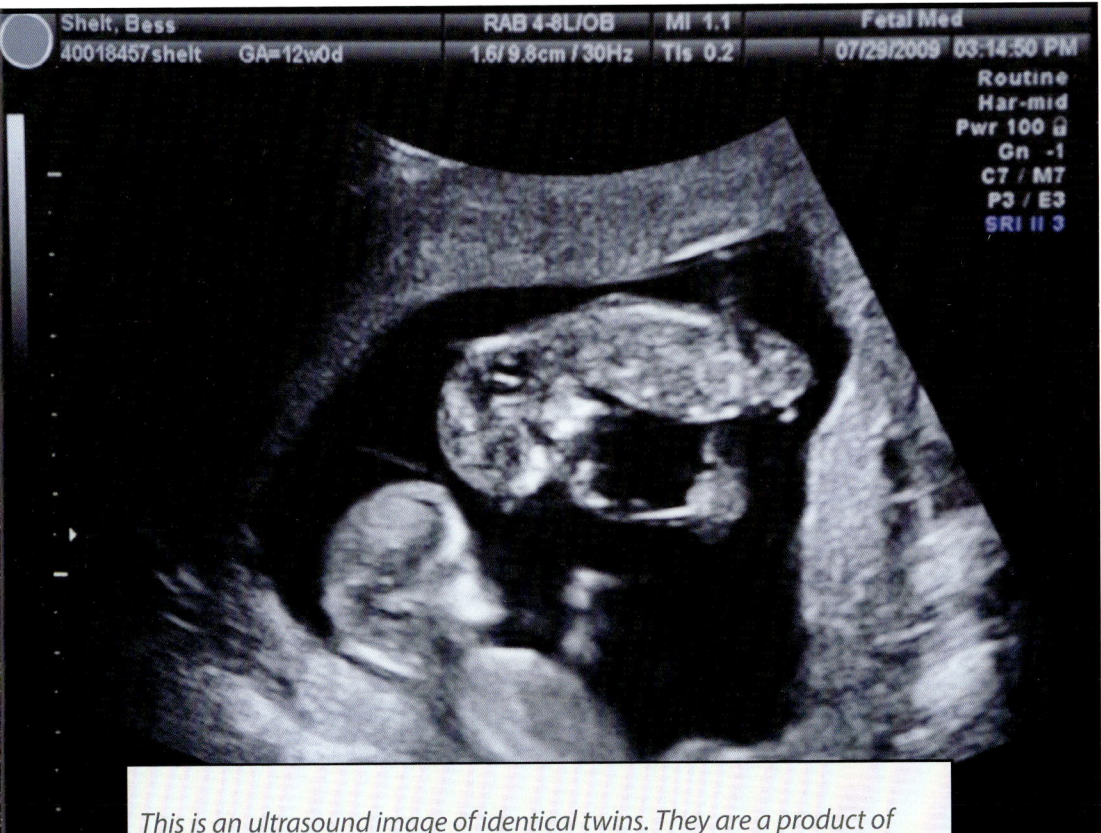

This is an ultrasound image of identical twins. They are a product of natural cloning. Tim Hale/Stone/Getty Images

twins. Mice are commonly cloned in this way to provide scientists with study subjects that have the same genetic constitution.

SOMATIC CELL NUCLEAR TRANSFER

With both blastomere separation and blastocyst division, the clone contains the genetic material from both a mother and father. In contrast, cloning via somatic cell nuclear transfer produces an embryo carrying the genetic material of only one parent. Scientists transfer the genetic material from a donor's somatic cell (any body cell other than a sex cell) to an egg cell that has had its own nucleus

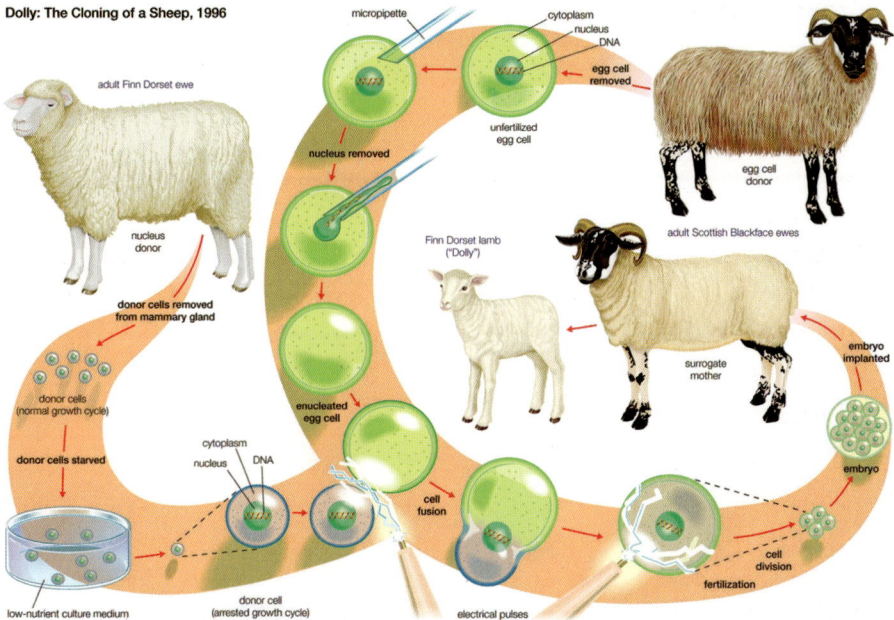

Dolly: The Cloning of a Sheep, 1996

This diagram shows how Dolly the sheep was cloned by fusing the nucleus from a mammary-gland cell of a Finn Dorset ewe into an enucleated egg cell from a Scottish Blackface ewe and then carried to term by another Scottish Blackface ewe. Encyclopaedia Britannica/Universal Images Group/Getty Images

and DNA removed. The resulting cloned cell contains the genetic material of the donor's somatic cell only.

Early somatic cell transfer experiments worked only when using cells from embryonic or immature animals. In 1996, however, British scientists successfully cloned a sheep named Dolly using adult somatic cells. With Dolly's birth, a new scientific path was discovered. Although undifferentiated embryonic cells were easier to work with, they could be unpredictable. After the Dolly experiment, scientists were better able to predict the physical characteristics of the clone because they were starting from an adult.

Although Dolly was not warmly received by much of the world, her existence, and the fact that she was later able to become pregnant and deliver her own offspring, is a testament to the medical promises inherent in cloning.

CONTROVERSY AND STEM CELL RESEARCH

Stem cells used in cytology and cloning have shown that they may also provide powerful information for additional biological research. In addition to being a catalyst for cloning, it is believed that stem cells could serve as starting points in the treatment of a wide variety of diseases, including Alzheimer's, Parkinson's, diabetes, and multiple sclerosis.

Some researchers believe that with enough time and attention, stem cell research could result not only in the ability to identify genetic indicators for various diseases, but provide more effective treatments for them, or even cures. However, the use of human embryonic stem cells evokes ethical concerns because

"ALIEN" DNA

In 2014, scientists were able to create an organism with artificial DNA. All life on Earth is based on the same genetic code. It is usually represented by the letters *A*, *C*, *G*, and *T*. The scientists created two additions to the genetic code and merged it with bacteria. The new codes were labeled *X* and *Y*. The new bacterium contained a six-letter genetic code rather than the four-letter code that occurs naturally. It opens up the possibility of different types of life-forms than what we know.

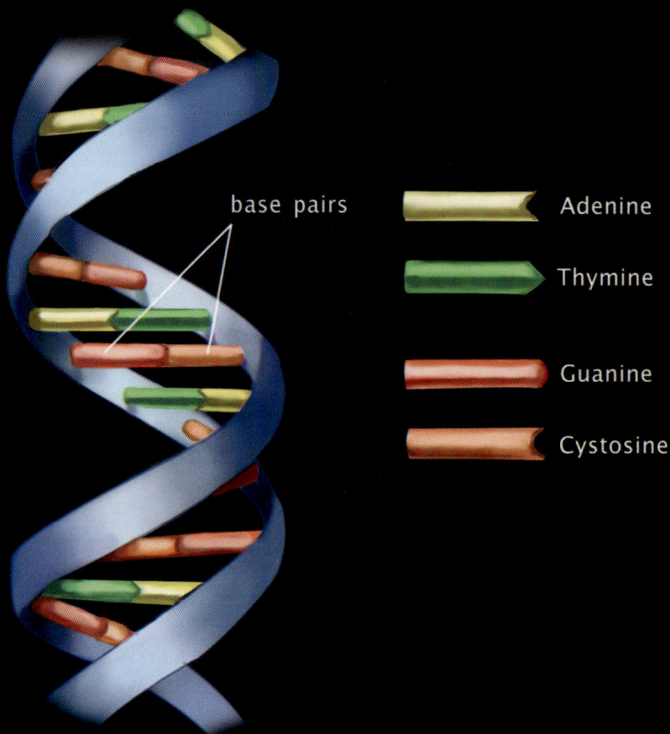

base pairs

Adenine

Thymine

Guanine

Cystosine

This illustration shows a DNA strand with combinations of base pairs coded with the letters A, C, G, and T. Scientists added two new codes, X and Y, to show other possibilities for life. Spencer Sutton/Science Source

the blastocyst-stage embryos are destroyed in the process of obtaining the stem cells. The embryos from which stem cells have been obtained are produced through in-vitro fertilization, and people who consider human embryos to be human beings generally believe that such work is morally wrong. Others accept it because they regard the blastocysts to be simply balls of cells, and human cells used in laboratories have not previously been given any special moral or legal

This researcher is viewing flourescent labeled stem cells. Rafe Swan/ Cultura/Getty Images

status. The controversy surrounding this issue is illustrated by the fact that the use of human embryonic stem cells is allowed in some countries and prohibited in others.

Due to the ethical and moral issues surrounding the use of embryonic stem cells, scientists have looked for ways to use adult cells. In 2012, the Nobel Prize in Medicine went to two scientists who programmed mature cells to become pluripotent (capable of differentiating into one of many cell types). Pluripotent cells usually come from unspecialized infant cells. However, the scientists were able to make mature cells differentiate, thus eliminating the need for controversial embryonic cells.

anaphase Phase of cell division when the paired chromosomes separate and move to opposite ends of the dividing cell.

asexual reproduction The division of a parent cell into two or more similar pieces, each of which becomes a new cell.

cell membrane Semipermeable outer layer of the cell body.

centromere The point at which two parts of a chromosome join, and at which the spindle fibers are attached during mitosis.

chromosome Threadlike structures in a cell's nucleus that carry DNA.

cleavage A series of early cell divisions of the fertilized ovum.

cloning A process that produces a cell, cell product, or organism that contains genetic material identical to the original.

cytokinesis The splitting of the cytoplasm into daughter cells following nuclear division.

cytology The study of plant and animal cells.

cytoplasm The jellylike interior of a cell.

differentiation A process by which cells become different and specialized.

DNA (deoxyribonucleic acid) The chemical basis of hereditary traits.

ectoderm The outermost layer of a group of cells, which will eventually develop into the skin, nervous system, and parts of the eye and inner ear.

embryo The developing organism, produced through sexual reproduction.

endoderm The middle layer of a group of cells, which will eventually develop into the internal organs.

endoplasmic reticulum A membranous organelle that forms a series of flattened sacs within the cytoplasm and is important in the synthesis, processing, and transport of proteins and lipids.

eukaryote A cell that contains a nucleus surrounded by a membrane.

gastrulation The process by which a fertilized egg becomes a multilayered embryo.

gene A unit of hereditary information stored within the cell's nucleus.

Golgi apparatus A membrane-bound organelle responsible for transporting, modifying, and packaging proteins and lipids for delivery to targeted destinations.

induction The process by which one cell or a set of cells influences the behavior of another cell or cells.

interphase A preliminary stage of cell division in which the cell grows and prepares for the actual division by first making a copy of its DNA.

meiosis The division process that produces cells with one-half the number of chromosomes in each daughter cell.

mesoderm The middle layer of a group of cells, which eventually develops into the heart, muscles, bones, blood, and sex organs.

metaphase The stage of mitosis or meiosis in which the chromatids line up along the equatorial plane in the middle of the cell.

mitochondria Oval-shaped organelles that serve as the site of cellular respiration to transform food molecules into energy.

mitosis The process of nuclear division producing a daughter cell with exactly the same number of chromosomes as in the parent cell.

nucleus Rounded structure inside a eukaryotic cell that is the cell's control center.

organogenesis A phase during cellular development when the embryo develops internal organs.

ovum A female sex cell, also known as the egg, produced by the female for sexual reproduction.

pluripotent Capable of differentiating into one of many cell types.

prokaryote A single-celled organism lacking a membrane-enclosed nucleus and organelles.

prophase The first phase of mitotic cell division, during which the chromosomes and spindles form between the cell's two centrioles.

protein Any naturally occurring, extremely complex substance that consists of amino-acid residues joined together by peptide bonds and contains the elements carbon, hydrogen, nitrogen, oxygen, usually sulfur, and other elements.

reproduction Creation of new life.

RNA (ribonucleic acid) A chemical that carries hereditary information and is involved in manufacturing proteins.

sexual reproduction The joining of gametes, or sex cells, to produce offspring.

stem cell Primitive, undifferentiated cells that have the potential to develop into any cells or tissues in the body.

telophase The final stage of mitosis, in which the nucleus of one cell is divided equally into two nuclei.

totipotent Capable of developing into a complete organism or differentiating into any of its cells or tissues, e.g. stem cells.

zygote A fertilized ovum.

FOR MORE INFORMATION

American Association for the Advancement of
Science (AAAS)
1200 New York Avenue NW
Washington, DC 20330
(202) 326-6400
Website: http://www.aaas.org
The American Association for the Advancement of Science
is a nonprofit international organization dedicated to
advancing science for humanity's benefit.

American Institute of Biological Sciences (AIBS)
1900 Campus Commons Drive, Suite 200
Reston, VA 20191
(703) 674-2500
Website: http://www.aibs.org
The American Institute of Biological Sciences is a scientific association that promotes biological
research and education for the betterment of
society. It publishes the peer-reviewed journal
BioScience and the education website
ActionBioscience.org.

American Society for Biochemistry and Molecular
Biology (ASBMB)
11200 Rockville Pike, Suite 302
Rockville, MD 20852-3110
(240) 283-6600
Website: http://www.asbmb.org
The American Society for Biochemistry and Molecular
Biology is dedicated to the advancement of

biochemistry and molecular biology. It publishes scientific and educational journals, organizes scientific meetings, and funds research and education in the field.

American Society for Cell Biology (ASCB)
8120 Woodmont Avenue, Suite 750
Bethesda, MD 20814-2762
(301) 347-9300
Website: http://www.ascb.org
The ASCB is an international community of cell biologists. They are committed to discovery, research, education, and professional development, as well as increasing diversity in the science community.

Canadian Society for Molecular Biosciences (CSMB)
c/o Rofail Conference and Management Services
17 Dossetter Way
Ottawa, ON K1G 4S3
Canada
(613) 421-7229
Website: http://www.csmb-scbm.ca
The Canadian Society for Molecular Biosciences was formed in 1957 to foster the science of biochemistry. The society established the Award of Excellence in 1976 to recognize major contributions in the field of genetics.

National Academy of Sciences (NAS)
500 Fifth Street NW
Washington, DC 20001

FOR FURTHER READING

Alberts, Bruce, Dennis Bray, Karen Hopkin, Alexander D. Johnson, Julian Lewis, Martin Raff, Keith Roberts, and Peter Walter. *Essential Cell Biology.* 4th ed. New York, NY: Garland Science, 2013.

Ballard, Carol. *Cells and Cell Function.* New York, NY: Rosen Publishing, 2010.

Goodsell, David S. *The Machinery of Life.* New York, NY: Copernicus Books, 2010.

Karp, Gerald. *Cell and Molecular Biology: Concepts and Experiments.* Hoboken, NJ: Wiley Publishing, 2013.

Keller, Rebecca W. *Focus on Middle School Biology.* Albequerque, NM: Gravitas Publications, 2012.

Stimola, Aubrey. *Cell Biology.* New York, NY: Rosen Publishing, 2011.

Tandon, Nina, and Mitchell Joachim. *Super Cells: Building with Biology.* New York, NY: TED Conferences, 2014.

Voet, Donald. *Fundamentals of Biochemistry: Life at the Molecular Level.* Hoboken, NJ: Wiley Publishing, 2012.

Wanjie, Anne. *The Basics of Cell Biology.* New York, NY: Rosen Publishing, 2014.

INDEX

A

adenosine triphosphate
(ATP), 12, 13, 17, 18
aerobic respiration,
12–13, 18
algae, 9, 12, 14
"alien" DNA, 50
Alzheimer's disease, 44, 49
American Society of Cell
Biology, 40
amino acids, 11
amniotic sacs, 34
amoebas, 7, 9, 42
anaerobic fermentation, 18
anaphase, 23–24, 25, 27
animal embryos, 33–36, 37,
38, 39, 46
apoptosis, 36
archaea, 8, 19
artificial specialization,
40–52
asexual reproduction, 21, 24
autotrophs, 14

B

bacteria, 4, 6, 7, 8, 19, 50
binary fission, 12, 19
blastocyst division, 46,
47–48

blastomere separation,
46–47, 48
blood cells, 4, 6, 29
Brown, Robert, 6

C

carbohydrates, 33
carbon dioxide, 12, 17
cells
division, 14, 19, 21–24
features of, 7–18
memory of, 42–44
overview, 4–6
reproduction, 9, 14,
21–28
specialized, 7, 29–39
centromeres, 23
centrosomes, 14
chlorophyll, 15, 17
chloroplasts, 12, 13, 15
chromatids, 23, 25, 28
chromatin, 24
chromosomes, 9, 14,
23–24, 25, 27, 28, 29
cleavage, 33, 34
cloning, 40, 41, 44–49
cytokinesis, 23, 24
cytology, 5, 6, 49
cytoplasm, 9, 10, 11, 24, 28
cytoskeleton, 40

D

deoxyribonucleic acid (DNA),
    8–9, 10, 11, 12, 13,
    20–21, 23, 24, 29, 30,
    49, 50
diabetes, 49
differentiation, 28, 29, 32–33,
    34, 41, 52
diploid cells, 25
Dolly the sheep, 49

E

E. B. Wilson Medal, 40
ectoderm, 34, 36
eggs, 7, 25, 28, 29, 30, 34,
    36, 38, 39, 46, 47, 48
embryos, 29, 33–39, 41, 42,
    46–47, 48, 49, 51, 52
endoderm, 34, 36
endoplasmic reticulum
    (ER), 11
endosymbiotic theory,
    12–13
enzymes, 14, 33
eukaryotes, 8, 9, 10, 18,
    19, 30

F

fermentation, 18
fertilization, 28, 29, 33, 34, 36,
    37, 46, 47, 51
fungi, 9

G

gastrulation, 33, 34, 36
genes, 21, 24, 29, 30, 32–33,
    37, 40, 42, 46, 48, 49,
    50
germination, 39
glucose, 12, 13, 17, 18
Golgi apparatus, 11

H

haploid cells, 25, 27, 28
heart disease, 44
Hooke, Robert, 5–6
hormones, 42
human embryos, 33, 36, 37,
    41, 51, 52

I

induction, 33
interphase, 23, 27

L

Leeuwenhoek, Antonie
    van, 6
lipids, 11, 14, 33
lysosomes, 12, 14

M

meiosis, 25–28
mesoderm, 34, 36

messenger RNA, 11
metaphase, 23, 25, 27
microscopes, 6
microtubules, 14
mitochondria, 11–12, 13,
        17–18
mitosis, 19, 21–24, 29, 44, 46
multiple sclerosis, 49
muscle cells, 7, 21, 42
mutations, 21, 33, 46

N

nerve cells, 7, 21, 29, 42
Nobel Prize, 40, 52
nucleus, 6, 8, 9, 10–11, 12,
        23, 24, 30, 32, 48

O

organelles, 8, 9, 10–12, 14
organogenesis, 33, 36, 38
ovum, 28
oxygen, 17, 18, 29

P

pancreatic cells, 42
paramecia, 9
Parkinson's disease, 44, 49
peroxisomes, 12, 14
photosynthesis, 12, 13,
        14–17
plant embryos, 38–39

pluripotent cells, 52
programmed cell death, 36
prokaryote, 8–9, 12, 13
prophase, 23, 25, 27
proteins, 11, 14, 21, 24, 29,
        30, 32, 33, 34
protozoa, 6

R

recombination, 25
reproduction, 9, 14, 21–28
respiration, 12, 13, 17–18
respiratory system, 4
ribonucleic acid (RNA), 11, 21
ribosomes, 9, 11, 12, 13, 21

S

Schleiden, Mathias, 6
Schwann, Theodor, 6
sexual reproduction, 24–28
skin cells, 7, 19
somatic cell nuclear transfer,
        46, 48–49
sperm, 28, 30, 38, 46
spindle fibers, 23, 24
stem cells, 29–30, 40, 41, 42,
        43, 49, 51–52
sugar, 11, 12, 17, 18

T

telophase, 23, 24, 25, 27
tetrads, 25
totipotent cells, 46

transcription factors, 30
transfer RNA, 11

U

undifferentiated cells, 29–30,
    40, 41, 46, 49, 51–52

Y

yeast, 4, 18
yolk sacs, 34

Z

zygotes, 29, 30, 32, 34, 38

(202) 334-2000
The NAS is a private, nonprofit society of scholars. It was created with the intent to provide independent, objective advice to the nation on anything related to science and technology.

National Institutes of Health (NIH)
9000 Rockville Pike
Bethesda, MD 20892
(301) 496-4000
Website: http://www.nih.gov
The NIH is part of the U.S. Department of Health and Human Services. It is the largest source of funding for medical research in the world, funding scientists around the United States and worldwide.

WEBSITES

Because of the changing nature of Internet links, Rosen Publishing has developed an online list of websites related to the subject of this book. This site is updated regularly. Please use this link to access this list:

http://www.rosenlinks.com/BGCB/Div